The Polar Bear Mystery

By Robert Kausal

Illlustrated by Luciana Navarro-Powell

Bill and Joe noticed the sign at the entrance to the zoo. The boys were at the zoo on a school field trip. As junior detectives it was their duty to help solve this mystery.

But first they needed to ask permission from their teacher. She shouted, "Lunch. 12:00 o'clock. Cafeteria. Be there or else!"

The boys arrived at the polar bear house. They saw a woman spraying the polar bear boulders with a hose.

"Excuse me, ma'am!" Bill shouted. "We'd like to ask you a few questions!" The boys quickly flashed their junior detective badges.

"Hey, I returned those movies last week!" the woman answered nervously.

"No, ma'am." Joe said. "This is about the missing polar bear."

"When was the last time you saw Scout?"
Bill asked.

"Last night," Zelda the zookeeper answered. "I
gave him two watermelons, and then I left."

Joe took out his notepad and pen. "What does
Scout look like?"

"White male, stands about six feet tall, and
has a long nose," Zelda answered.

"That sounds like half the people in this city!"
Joe exclaimed.

4

Zelda reached into her pocket and gave the boys a picture of Scout. "This is Scout and I. I'm the one cleaning the boulder," she said.

Bill noticed Zelda's black raincoat in the picture. "How come you're not wearing your raincoat?" Bill asked.

"I don't know what happened to it," said Zelda.

"Hmmm," Bill said. "We'll be in touch."

The boys studied their notes. Suddenly, Bill stopped. "Look!" he shouted.

"Some litterbug threw snow-cone cups on the sidewalk!" Joe yelled.

"No, not that," Bill said, pointing. "That!" Black watermelon seeds dotted the sidewalk. "Are you thinking what I'm thinking?"

"It's lunchtime?" Joe guessed.

"No," Bill said. "Those are watermelon seeds. Follow the seeds and we find Scout!"

The boys followed the seeds all the way to the entrance of Penguin World. It's where the penguins lived.

Something wasn't right. A large group of penguins was huddled together in the corner. They looked frightened. They were shaking and chirping loudly. And on top of the snow-covered hill was the largest penguin the boys had ever seen.

"That's one huge penguin!" Joe exclaimed.

Bill looked closely at the large penguin that was sliding down the hill. "That's no penguin!" Bill shouted. "That's Scout!" Scout was wearing Zelda's black raincoat and a snow-cone cup on his nose. He looked just like a penguin . . . sort of.

"Let's go find Zelda! Another case solved for the junior detectives!" Bill said.